I'm special

WAYLAND

Your Feelings

I'm lonely	I'm happy
I'm worried	I feel bullied
It's not fair	I'm special
I'm shy	

First published in 1999 by Wayland Publishers Ltd
This edition published in 2001 and reprinted in 2003 and 2004
by Hodder Wayland, an imprint of Hodder Children's Books
Reprinted in 2006 by Wayland, an imprint of Hachette Children's Books

 Find out about how this book is relevant to
the National Literacy Strategy on page 31.

Designer: Jean Wheeler
Consultant: Nick Tapp, Deputy Chief Executive, East Sussex
Disability Association

British Library Cataloguing in Publication Data
  Green, Jen, 1955-
  I'm special. - (Your feelings)
  1. Handicapped - Juvenile literature
  I.Title
  362.4

ISBN-10: 0-7502-2575-0
ISBN-13: 978-0-7502-2575-5

Typeset by Jean Wheeler
Printed in China by WKT Company Ltd

Hachette Children's Books
338 Euston Road, London NW1 3BH

I'm special

Written by Jen Green

Illustrated by Mike Gordon

WAYLAND

My name is Sarah. You could say I'm special. My legs don't work properly, so I use a wheelchair to get about.

I love music, and play the recorder in our school orchestra.

I love animals,
especially our cat
and dog.

My best friend Jo is also special. She's a whizz at maths and science.

She can't see well, but her calculator speaks to her out loud.

Our friend Ben is special too. He's the champion swimmer in our class.

Ben can't hear much. He has a hearing aid.

8

He watches people's lips
to find out what
they are saying.

When people stare or point at me as I go by, I feel shy.

10

Sometimes I think they are scared because I am special, not quite the same as them.

When people talk to Jo as if she's stupid, she feels upset.

She can't see well, but she's just as quick as them.

When other kids tease Ben behind his back so he can't hear them, he feels angry.

But he talks in signs to
his friend Jeff instead.

When my brother leaves me out of games like football, I feel sad.

Last week when I played with the others, I scored a goal!

When grown-ups ignore me and talk to Mum as if I wasn't there, I feel cross.

'Ask me!
I can speak
for myself,
you know!'

When buildings have so many stairs I can't go in, I feel left out.

But the new sports centre has lifts and ramps, and we have great fun there.

Some grown-ups I know
are special too. They all
seem very busy.

Hannah's mum has a wheelchair ...

and drives a fast, shiny car.

Mrs Mills, from our street, is the boss of a big office.

Mr Black is the head teacher at our school.

When grown-ups fuss and try to
help with something I can do,
I feel embarrassed.

It's OK when children who are special take longer to do something, or do it in a different way.

Often I like to be treated just the same as everyone else.

Everyone finds some things hard
and some things easy.

Everyone is different and special,
just like me.

Notes for parents and teachers

This book provides an introduction to the subject of disability for young children. Parents or teachers who have read the book with children, either individually or in groups, may find it useful to stop and discuss issues as they come up.

Ask children to name all the different kinds of disability they can think of. Talk about different disabilities, including mental disabilities. Encourage children to imagine what it is like to be disabled by making their way from the blackboard to their desk blindfold, or by trying to understand the lesson while covering their ears. Ask children to do a survey of their home, classroom or the whole school, making a list of the difficulties that would be encountered by a child in a wheelchair. (Are there many stairs? Are pegs, lockers and other facilities at the right height? Are toilets accessible?) Talk about ways in which buildings can be changed to make things easier for disabled people.

This book describes a number of attitudes and reactions that people with disabilities encounter frequently. Common reactions include staring, ignoring disabled people, providing help before asking if any is needed, and making assumptions or patronising comments. Explain that many disabled people feel their biggest disadvantage is other people's attitudes towards them. Encourage the children to act out real or imaginary encounters between disabled and able-bodied children. Then suggest that children exchange roles. How would they feel if they were treated as disabled people often are? How would they resolve the situation? Other children can comment on whether the scenes acted out were realistic or not.

Alternatively, children may like to write list poems that explore the feelings of people with disabilities:

When I can't see the new film at the cinema because there are too many stairs, I feel left out.

When you shout at me as if I'm stupid, I feel hurt and angry.

Explore the fact that sometimes people try to insult others by using words that describe people with various disabilities. Explain that name-calling is cruel and hurtful, like racism. Children may decide that name-calling is not acceptable, and that they will challenge it. Parents can help by exploring their own attitudes to disability, and realizing that their attitudes influence their children.

Use this book for teaching literacy

This book can help you in the literacy hour in the following ways:

- ✓ Children can write simple stories linked to personal experience using the language of the text in this book as a model for their own writing. (Year 1, Term 3: Non-fiction writing composition)

- ✓ Children can look through the book and try to locate verbs with past and present tense endings. (Year 1, Term 3: Word recognition, graphic knowledge and spelling)

- ✓ Use of speech bubbles and enlarged print shows different ways of presenting texts. (Year 2, Term 2: Sentence construction and punctuation)

Books to read

Don't Call Me Special by Pat Thomas and Lesley Harker (Hodder Wayland 2005)
A delightful picture book for young children which explores questions and concerns about disability in a simple and reassuring way.

Flop-Ear by Guido Van Genechten (Franklin Watts, 2001)
All the other rabbits make fun of Flop-Ear whose right ear insists on drooping down no matter what he does. A picture book tale about Flop-Ear's attempts to be like everyone else and his eventual acceptance that he is different.

See You Tomorrow Charles by Miriam Cohen and Lillian Hoban (Random House,1989) When Charles, a young blind boy, joins his new class Anna Maria and the other children feel unsure of themselves and of him until they learn to accept Charles.

Something Else by Kathryn Cave and Chris Riddell (Puffin 1995).
This is a simple story about a creature called Something Else who is excluded from his neighbour's activities because he behaves and looks different. But then when a stranger creature tries to make friends with Something Else, he doesn't want to know until he sees himself in the mirror.